U.S. HISTORY TIMELINES

First Settlers
1492-1607

Simon Rose

www.av2books.com

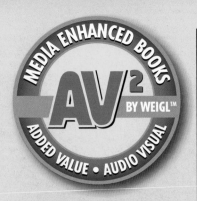

AV² provides enriched content that supplements and complements this book. Weigl's AV² books strive to create inspired learning and engage young minds in a total learning experience.

Your AV² Media Enhanced books come alive with...

Audio
Listen to sections of the book read aloud.

Key Words
Study vocabulary, and complete a matching word activity.

Video
Watch informative video clips.

Quizzes
Test your knowledge.

Embedded Weblinks
Gain additional information for research.

Slide Show
View images and captions, and prepare a presentation.

Try This!
Complete activities and hands-on experiments.

... and much, much more!

Go to **www.av2books.com**, and enter this book's unique code.

BOOK CODE

K932796

AV² **by Weigl** brings you media enhanced books that support active learning.

Published by AV² by Weigl
350 5th Avenue, 59th Floor
New York, NY 10118
Websites: www.av2books.com   www.weigl.com

Library of Congress Cataloging-in-Publication Data available upon request.

ISBN 978-1-4896-0704-1 (hardcover)
ISBN 978-1-4896-0705-8 (softcover)
ISBN 978-1-4896-0706-5 (single-user eBook)
ISBN 978-1-4896-0707-2 (multi-user eBook)

Printed in the United States of America in North Mankato, Minnesota
1 2 3 4 5 6 7 8 9 0   18 17 16 15 14

052014
WEP301113

Editor: Pamela Dell
Project Coordinator: Aaron Carr
Designer: Mandy Christiansen

Every reasonable effort has been made to trace ownership and to obtain permission to reprint copyright material. The publishers would be pleased to have any errors or omissions brought to their attention so that they may be corrected in subsequent printings.

Weigl acknowledges Getty Images as its primary image supplier for this title.

CONTENTS

In the Beginning

Explorer Christopher Columbus set out from Spain in August 1492. Funded by that country's king and queen, he traveled west across the Atlantic Ocean. Columbus expected to reach Asia. Instead, he arrived in the "New World" on October 12 of that year.

This **voyage** gave Spain a head start in the race to claim new lands. Portugal was close behind. Later, other European nations followed.

For the next 100 years, European interest in **colonizing** the New World grew. The early settlers fought each other for land. They also fought with the native peoples already living on the land. It was just the beginning of the vast change coming to North America.

QUEEN ISABELLA AND King Ferdinand II of Spain provided Christopher Columbus with three ships for his journey.

1492
1494
1493–1496
1497–1507
1513–1532
1524–1540
1540–1542

EPIDEMICS AND DISEASE

The native peoples of the New World had no **immunity** to diseases carried by the Europeans. Thousands of American Indians died from such diseases. Some of these included smallpox, typhus, and measles. More died of disease than were killed fighting the invaders.

LA ISABELA

In January 1494, on his second voyage, Columbus founded a **settlement** called La Isabela on the island he called Hispaniola. Named after Spain's queen, La Isabela was located on the northern coast of the island. The settlement was abandoned four years later.

Today, the countries of Haiti and the Dominican Republic share the island of Hispaniola. A church marks the spot where Columbus created this settlement so long ago.

TREATY OF TORDESILLAS

In 1494, Spain and Portugal agreed to the **Treaty** of Tordesillas. This treaty officially divided the newly discovered lands beyond Europe. The division line ran through the Atlantic Ocean 1,099 miles (1,770 kilometers) west of the Cape Verde Islands near Africa.

Spain received all the territory west of the line. Portugal claimed all new lands to the east. This gave most of the Americas to Spain, but Portugal gained the present-day country of Brazil.

The Continuing Voyages of Columbus

Between 1493 and 1504, Columbus made three more trips to North America. On his first voyage, he had explored some of the **Caribbean** islands, including today's Cuba. He returned to Spain in March 1493.

On November 3, 1493, Columbus arrived back in the New World. On this trip, he brought about 1,500 men with him. Spain had paid for this bigger **expedition** for good reason. This time, Columbus expected to find gold and return with riches for Spain.

In the islands, however, Columbus found little gold. Angered, the Spaniards committed brutal acts against the native peoples living there. Some had their hands cut off. Hundreds were enslaved. Columbus returned to Spain in June 1496. All he had to show for his efforts were 300 enslaved Indians he had brought back. Queen Isabella was shocked. Spain wanted no part in slavery.

SANTO DOMINGO, THE current capital of the Dominican Republic, was founded in 1496 by Columbus's brother Bartholomew. It is the oldest continuously occupied European settlement in the Americas.

As an explorer, Columbus hoped to find a fast route to Asia by traveling west from Europe. On reaching North America, Columbus mistakenly believed he had discovered islands off the coast of India. For this reason, he called the native peoples "Indians."

Exploration Expands

Columbus's third voyage went from 1498 to 1500. This time, he explored mainland South America. Columbus made his final voyage between 1502 and 1504. On this trip, he reached the present-day countries of Mexico, Honduras, Panama, and Jamaica.

Soon, other explorers were voyaging to the New World. Amerigo Vespucci explored the coast of South America for Spain and Portugal. Great Britain sent Italian explorer John Cabot across the Atlantic as well.

In 1497, Cabot explored the coast of Canada, including Labrador and Newfoundland. Like others, he hoped to discover the "Northwest Passage." If such a water route across North America existed, it would provide a shorter route to Asia.

Discoveries made in the New World encouraged more explorers. In the following decades, many would cross the Atlantic to claim land and search for gold and other riches.

JOHN CABOT WAS born in Genoa, Italy, as Giovanni Caboto. In 1497, he landed in what is now eastern Canada. Cabot led a larger expedition in 1498. He made the first claims to North America on behalf of England.

AMERIGO VESPUCCI WAS an Italian explorer. He was the first European explorer to realize that the newly discovered lands were not part of Asia but a whole new continent. In 1507, the first map was printed that named the new lands Vespucci had found. They were called "America" in his honor.

Spanish Explorers and Conquerors

The Spanish were among the first Europeans to explore the New World. In 1513, Ponce de León became the first European to land in Florida. Further south, Hernán Cortés arrived in Mexico in 1519. There, he **conquered** the Aztec Empire for Spain. Also in 1519, Domenico de Pineda explored the Gulf of Mexico. Two years later, Francisco de Gordillo explored the Atlantic coast as far north as present-day South Carolina.

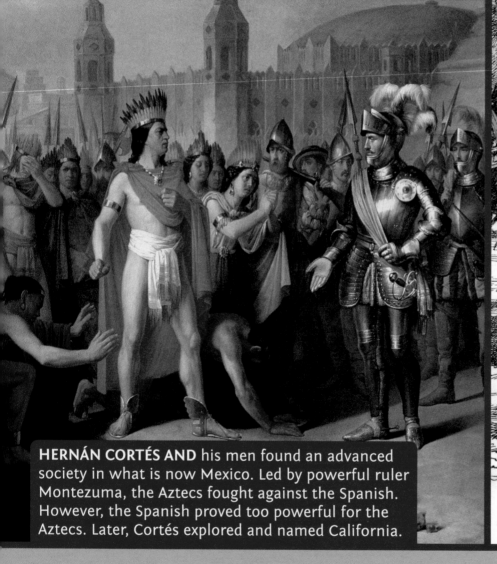

HERNÁN CORTÉS AND his men found an advanced society in what is now Mexico. Led by powerful ruler Montezuma, the Aztecs fought against the Spanish. However, the Spanish proved too powerful for the Aztecs. Later, Cortés explored and named California.

1492–1494	1493–1496	1497–1507	1513	1524–1540	1540–1542
○	○	○	★	○	○
			1532		

ON FIRST SIGHT, the Aztecs were afraid of the horses the Spanish rode. They thought the strange animals were large deer.

THE SPANISH CONQUISTADORES

Spanish *conquistadores*, or conquerors, were driven by power and gold. Hernán Cortés was one of the most successful of the conquistadores Spain sent to claim new lands. Cortés landed in Mexico with just 500 men. He soon led his army against the Aztec Empire of modern-day Mexico. By 1921, Cortés had overthrown the Aztecs and took control of their gold and silver mines for Spain.

Though the Aztecs had greater numbers, the Spanish had more advanced weapons and armor. The Spanish also had horses.

In 1532, Francisco Pizarro led another Spanish expedition into South America. Pizarro overthrew the Inca Empire and further strengthened Spain's control in the New World.

Further Exploration

In 1524, France sent Italian Giovanni da Verrazzano to explore the Atlantic coast from present-day North Carolina to Maine. More Europeans soon to followed. Between 1528 and 1536, Álvar Núñez Cabeza de Vaca of Spain became the first European to explore the American Southwest. He explored parts of modern-day Texas, New Mexico, and Arizona. Cabeza De Vaca also explored parts of northern Mexico. In 1540, Francisco Vázquez de Coronado led an expedition into the Southwest. One of the men with him, Garcia López de Cárdenas, became the first European to see the Grand Canyon.

1492–1494	1493–1496	1497–1507	1513–1532	1524	1540–1542

1540

ÁLVAR NÚÑEZ CABEZA DE VACA

Álvar Núñez Cabeza de Vaca suffered one disaster after another. After being shipwrecked off the coast of today's Texas in 1528, he spent nearly seven years among the American Indians. From Texas, he made his way down the coast and inland to Mexico City.

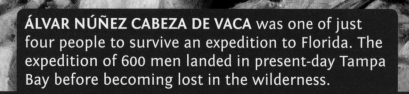

ÁLVAR NÚÑEZ CABEZA DE VACA was one of just four people to survive an expedition to Florida. The expedition of 600 men landed in present-day Tampa Bay before becoming lost in the wilderness.

Exploring the Southwest

In the late 1530s and early 1540s, the Spanish explored much of North America's southern half. Hernando de Soto explored Florida and what would become the southeastern United States. He also explored the mouth of the Mississippi River in 1541.

In 1540, Francisco Vázquez de Coronado traveled north from Mexico into the American Southwest. He was in search of gold and other treasures. His two-year expedition took him at least as far as central Kansas. Some of his men were the first Europeans to see the Grand Canyon. Farther west, Juan Rodríguez Cabrillo became the first European to explore the coast of California in 1542.

HERNANDO DE SOTO died of a fever in Louisiana in 1542. He was buried on the banks of the Mississippi River, which he had explored.

De Soto had been part of Francisco Pizarro's expedition to South America in the early 1530s. There, they conquered Peru's Inca Empire.

GREED FOR GOLD

The Spanish conquistadores were driven by tales of great riches hidden in the New World. Many hunted for the so-called seven Golden Cities of Cibola but found nothing. Some explorers did strike it rich in the New World, however. Hernando de Soto was one of them.

FRANCISCO VÁZQUEZ DE CORONADO

Vázquez de Coronado wanted to find the cities of gold. His expedition included some 300 soldiers and hundreds of American Indians. They explored modern-day Arizona, New Mexico, Texas, Oklahoma, and Kansas. One of his men spotted the Grand Canyon, but the explorers never found Golden Cities of Cibola.

The First American Colonies

Both Spain and France tried to start colonies in Florida and on the Atlantic coast. The 1559 Spanish settlement at Pensacola, Florida, did not survive. A French colony in South Carolina failed in 1562.

Some French Huguenots, treated badly at home because of their religious beliefs, fled to northern Florida. There, they started a colony called Fort Caroline in 1564.

A year later, the Spanish settled in nearby St. Augustine. In September 1565, Pedro Menéndez de Avilés led a brutal attack on Fort Caroline. The Spaniards killed all but 60 women and children. They renamed the colony Fort Mateo. In 1568, the French destroyed Fort Mateo.

PEDRO MENÉNDEZ DE AVILÉS was the first colonial governor of Florida. He built watchtowers at Biscayne Bay and Cape Canaveral in present-day Florida.

1492–1494   1493–1496   1497–1507   1513–1532   1524–1540   1540–1542

THE HUGUENOTS

The Huguenots were French Protestants. In Europe during the 1500s, followers of the Protestant religion and followers of the Catholic religion were enemies. Many Huguenots left France and settled in other European countries. Some sought their fortune in the New World.

ST. AUGUSTINE

St. Augustine, Florida, is the oldest continuously occupied city in the United States. It was an important Spanish post during the colonial period.

St. Augustine was a base for guarding Spanish trade ships that sailed back and forth between Europe and North America.

SPANISH KING PHILIP II ordered Menéndez to attack Fort Caroline. Spain had claimed the land and did not want others trying to take it.

English Claims

In the late 1570s and early 1580s, Britain put great effort into New World exploration. English explorers Sir Martin Frobisher and Sir Humphrey Gilbert both made voyages in search of the Northwest Passage.

Sir Francis Drake was the first English citizen to successfully **circumnavigate** the world. This journey lasted from 1577 to 1580. During the voyage, Drake attacked Spanish ships and territory. He landed in northern California in 1579. Claiming the area for English Queen Elizabeth I, he named it Nova Albion.

DRAKE SUCCESSFULLY BATTLED Spanish ships in Europe as well as in South America. The riches he took from surrendered ships made him wealthy.

Sir Francis Drake set out on his trip around the world with five ships. Only his own, the *Golden Hind*, made it back to England. On his return in 1581, Queen Elizabeth **knighted** Drake on the ship's deck. He became a national hero after battling the powerful **Spanish Armada** in 1588. Drake died on January 28, 1596, off the coast of Panama. His death was caused by illness. Drake's body was buried at sea.

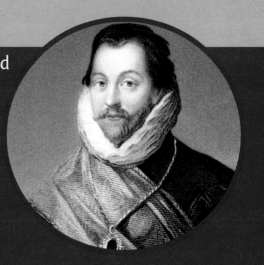

SIR FRANCES DRAKE changed the ship's name from the *Pelican* to the *Golden Hind* when he sailed through the Strait of Magellen.

The Lost Colony

In July 1587, 117 English settlers landed on Roanoke Island in what is now North Carolina. Sir Walter Raleigh had organized the expedition to claim land for Britain and start a colony.

That same year, the colony leader, John White, sailed back to England for fresh supplies. He did not make it back to Roanoke until 1590. Upon his return, he found no sign of the colonists. The letters "CRO" were carved into a tree, and the word "CROATOAN" was carved into a gatepost.

ONE REASON for John White's delayed return was the war Britain was fighting with Spain. At Roanoke, he found nothing but the "Croatoan" clue. What did it mean? At the time, "Croatoan" was the name for nearby Hatteras Island.

Sir Walter Raleigh (1554–1618) was an English explorer. He led expeditions to South America in search of gold. He also organized expeditions to colonize the eastern coast of North America during the 1580s. He was a favorite of Queen Elizabeth I. In 1618, however, Raleigh was executed for **treason** by the queen's successor, King James I.

THE FATE OF THE COLONISTS

What became of the Roanoke colonists is still a mystery. American Indians or the Spanish may have killed them. They may have joined with the native peoples and intermarried. Some historians believe the colonists died of starvation or disease. Others think they may have been lost at sea during an attempt to return to England.

VIRGINIA DARE

Virginia Dare was the first child born in the Americas to English parents. She was born on August 18, 1587, in the Roanoke Colony.

First Permanent Settlements

By the late 1500s, Europeans had established permanent settlements in North America. In 1598, Don Juan de Oñate claimed New Mexico for Spain. Oñate named the capital San Juan de los Caballeros. Near present-day Santa Fe, it was the first permanent European settlement in the West.

The first permanent French colony in North America was settled by Samuel de Champlain in 1605. That settlement was Port Royal in what is now Nova Scotia, Canada. This became the capital of the French colony of Acadia.

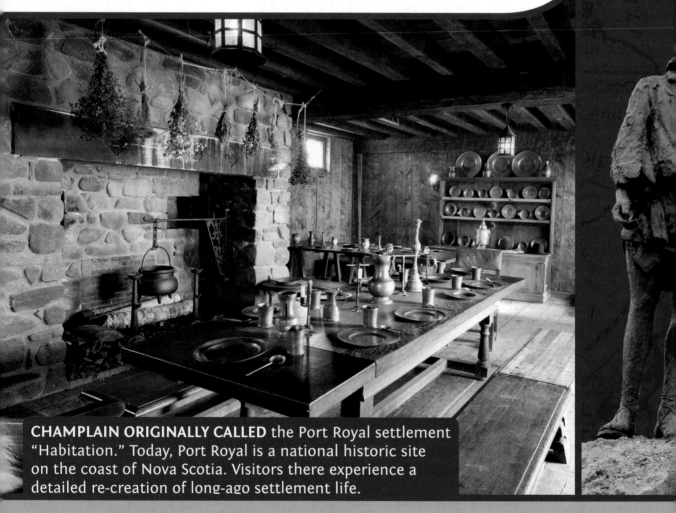

CHAMPLAIN ORIGINALLY CALLED the Port Royal settlement "Habitation." Today, Port Royal is a national historic site on the coast of Nova Scotia. Visitors there experience a detailed re-creation of long-ago settlement life.

1492–1494   1493–1496   1497–1507   1513–1532   1524–1540   1540–1542

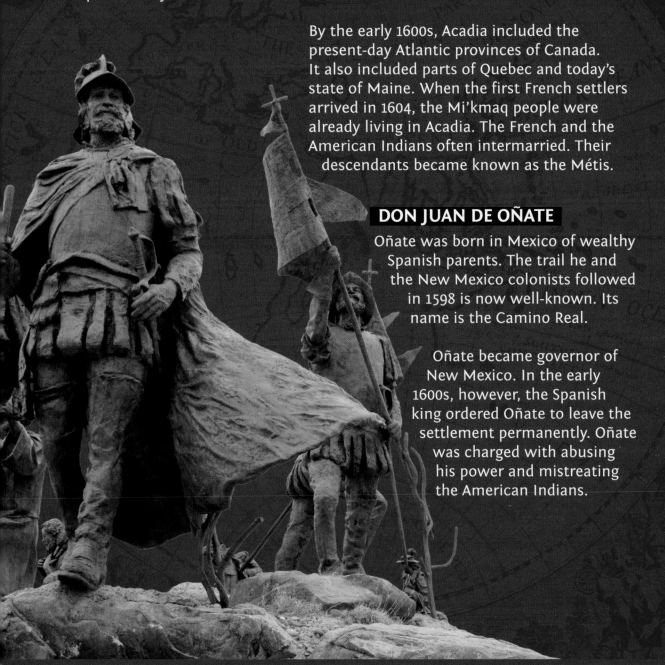

ACADIA

In 1524, Italian explorer Giovanni da Verrazzano sailed for North America. France's King Francis I had sent him to search for the Northwest Passage. Verrazzano explored America's northeast Atlantic coast. He called the area near present-day Delaware "Arcadia," which later became "Acadia."

By the early 1600s, Acadia included the present-day Atlantic provinces of Canada. It also included parts of Quebec and today's state of Maine. When the first French settlers arrived in 1604, the Mi'kmaq people were already living in Acadia. The French and the American Indians often intermarried. Their descendants became known as the Métis.

DON JUAN DE OÑATE

Oñate was born in Mexico of wealthy Spanish parents. The trail he and the New Mexico colonists followed in 1598 is now well-known. Its name is the Camino Real.

Oñate became governor of New Mexico. In the early 1600s, however, the Spanish king ordered Oñate to leave the settlement permanently. Oñate was charged with abusing his power and mistreating the American Indians.

The Virginia Colony

In 1606, Britain's King James I issued the First Virginia **Charter**. This created the Virginia Company. The company's purpose was to colonize the area known as Virginia, along North America's Atlantic coast.

The first colonists arrived at Jamestown, Virginia, in 1607. Theirs was the first permanent English settlement in the New World. Later, more English colonies sprang up along the East Coast. These colonies would eventually become the first U.S. states.

THE VIRGINIA COLONY was one of 13 English colonies that later became the United States. Each colony was part of a larger group. These groups were known as the southern colonies, the middle colonies, and the New England colonies.

A LARGER VIRGINIA

In 1606, the area called Virginia stretched along the east coast of North America from South Carolina to Canada.

HONORING THE QUEEN

Virginia was named in honor of Queen Elizabeth I, known as the Virgin Queen. Her reign lasted from 1558 until her death in 1603.

QUEEN ELIZABETH I was a powerful monarch. She ruled England for 45 years.

The Brink of Change

Many new European colonies were set up in the 1500s and 1600s. This brought great change in the New World.

Some of these early settlements failed, but many were successful. In the 1600s and 1700s, more and more people crossed the Atlantic to start a new life in America. The European nations continued to expand their North American empires. Sometimes, they waged war to defend their interests.

This fighting among nations often involved American Indians as well. The conflicts pitted native peoples against one side or the other, and sometimes against each other. Over time, as European colonization spread.

1492–1494   1493–1496   1497–1507   1513–1532   1524–1540   1540–1542

THE AMERICAN INDIANS struggled to preserve their way of life. European settlement was not about to stop, however. Conflicts that arose between the two groups were often violent.

Activity

Fill in the Blanks

Timelines are only a beginning. They provide an overview of the key events and important people that shaped history. Now, research in the library and on the internet to discover the rest of the story of the earliest settlements in America.

Use a concept web to organize your ideas. Use the questions in the concept web to guide your research. When finished, use the completed web to help you write your report.

QUEEN ISABELLA of Spain eagerly greeted Christopher Columbus when he returned from his first voyage to the New World.

Concept Web

Important Events
- What significant events shaped the times or the person you're writing about?
- Were there any major events that triggered some turning point in the life or the time you are writing about?

Key People
- Discuss one or two main figures who had an impact on the times, event, or person you are researching.
- What negative or positive actions by people had a lasting effect on history?

Historic Places
- Discuss some of the most important places related to the subject of your research.
- Are there some important places that are not well-known today?
- If so, what are they and why were they important at the time or to your subject?

Causes
- How was your subject affected by important historical moments of the time?
- Was there any chain of events to cause a particular outcome in the event, time, or the life you are researching?

Write a History Report

Obstacles
- What were some of the most difficult moments or events in the life of the person or in the historical timeline of the topic you are researching?
- Were there any particular people who greatly aided in the overcoming of obstacles?

Outcome and Lasting Effects
- What was the outcome of this chain of events?
- Was there a lasting effect on your subject?
- What is the importance of these "stepping stones" of history? How might the outcome have changed if things had happened differently?

Into the Future
- What lasting impact did your subject have on history?
- Is that person, time, or event well-known today?
- Have people's attitudes changed from back then until now about your subject?
- Do people think differently today about the subject than they did at the time the event happened or the person was alive?

Brain Teaser

1. Who was the first Englishman to sail around the world?

2. During what years did Columbus make his second voyage to North America?

3. Where was the Lost Colony?

4. What is the name of the water route that Europeans believed would be a shortcut across North America to the Pacific Ocean?

5. Which treaty divided the New World between Spain and Portugal?

6. Who was the first European to see the Grand Canyon?

7. What was the first permanent French settlement in North America?

8. Who was the first child born in the Americas to English parents?

9. Who discovered the mouth of the Mississippi River in 1541?

10. What is the oldest continuously occupied city in the United States?

ANSWERS

1. Sir Francis Drake
2. 1493 to 1496
3. Roanoke Island
4. The Northwest Passage
5. The Treaty of Tordesillas
6. García López de Cárdenas
7. Port Royal
8. Virginia Dare
9. Hernando de Soto
10. St. Augustine, Florida

Key Words

Caribbean: an area of the Atlantic Ocean between North and South America

charter: an official document outlining rules and regulations

circumnavigate: to travel around the entire world

colonizing: taking control of a distant territory by sending settlers there

conquered: forcefully gained control of territory, usually by war

expedition: a journey undertaken with a clear objective

immunity: ability to resist a disease

knighted: specially honored by a English ruler for some outstanding deed, giving a man the title of "Sir" before his name

settlement: a small community usually set up by people from another place

Spanish Armada: Spain's large fleet of ships in the 1500s, which was sent to invade Britain in 1588

treason: the act of betraying one's country

treaty: a formal agreement between two or more countries

voyage: a long journey to a distant place, usually used for ocean travel

Index

Log on to www.av2books.com

AV² by Weigl brings you media enhanced books that support active learning. Go to www.av2books.com, and enter the special code found on page 2 of this book. You will gain access to enriched and enhanced content that supplements and complements this book. Content includes video, audio, weblinks, quizzes, a slide show, and activities.

AV² Online Navigation

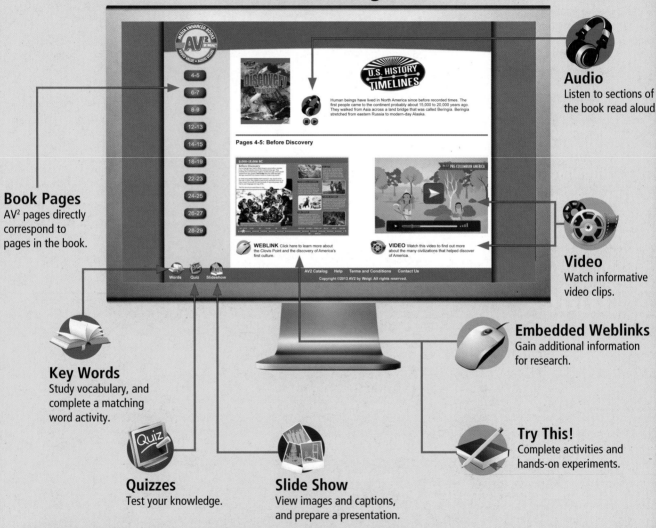

Audio
Listen to sections of the book read aloud

Book Pages
AV² pages directly correspond to pages in the book.

Video
Watch informative video clips.

Key Words
Study vocabulary, and complete a matching word activity.

Embedded Weblinks
Gain additional information for research.

Try This!
Complete activities and hands-on experiments.

Quizzes
Test your knowledge.

Slide Show
View images and captions, and prepare a presentation.

AV² was built to bridge the gap between print and digital. We encourage you to tell us what you like and what you want to see in the future.

Sign up to be an AV² Ambassador at www.av2books.com/ambassador.

Due to the dynamic nature of the Internet, some of the URLs and activities provided as part of AV² by Weigl may have changed or ceased to exist. AV² by Weigl accepts no responsibility for any such changes. All media enhanced books are regularly monitored to update addresses and sites in a timely manner. Contact AV² by Weigl at 1-866-649-3445 or av2books@weigl.com with any questions, comments, or feedback.